The Devil's
Heart

TABLE OF CONTENTS

ABSTRACT

Sandra, a young lady from a wealthy family background got admitted into the university of Benin, only to be introduced to a different world entirely where power is coveted and brutality is a weapon of maintaining power. long the way, She was caught in-between the web of love of two gladiators in the dark world, Adex, the one who once saved her and Collins, the one who appears to be a perfect gentle man.

After falling in love with Sandra, Adex and Collins path begin to differ as Sandra's love made Adex to lose his brutality which led to the loss of his power but Collins would continued his ruthless life. He won with Adex but had a bigger obstacle in his way in order to win Sandra and that Obstacle is Segun, the one Sandra truly loves. Fuel by his greed and desire to get everything that he wants, Collins would do anything until he met someone who has more greed than him, Cindy.

CHAPTER ONE

A NEW WORLD

'The class ended fifteen minutes ago and you are still staring into the blank air. I hope all is well with you'. Mariam one of Sandra's course mate reached out to her. Sandra couldn't believe that she had gone that far , deep in her thoughts. 'I am fine, thanks!' She said forging a smile on her face.

Many thoughts ran through her mind as she packed her books into her bag. She wasn't sure if she still wants to fight on or if she should just end it all. She lifted her legs which seemed to be heavy, but she continued to walk towards the exit of the hall. 'Are you sure that you are fine? ' Mariam, who had been staring at her for a while asked. Sandra blurted out another smile, a smile that any witty person would be sure wasn't genuine. 'Try to visit the clinic if you are not well.' 'yes, I will, thanks.'

As she trekked towards the exit of the gate, beholding the bea utiful flowers that makes the school the pride of the nation. Even in her depressed state she couldn't help but smile at the memory of her admission into the school. Unfortunately, it was the beginning of her pain or let me say, the beginning of her great dilemma.

Two years ago, Sandra got admitted into the un iversity of Benin. She was so excited when she received her admission le tter, she rushed into her mother's room to share the good news with her. Finally, her daughter has made her proud. Tears rolled down Mama Sandra's face as she stared at her very excited daughter. 'Mama, why are you crying?' Sandra asked after she noticed the water flooding out of her mother's wrinkled eyes. 'My daughter, it is a tear of Joy, finally, you will able to fulfill your dream of becoming an accountant.' Sandra gave her mother a tight hug as tears escaped from her eyes. It was an emotional day. Mama Sandra wasn't crying just because her daughter had gained admission, she was crying because, it has become a thing of ridicule for her before her friends wh o would always boast of their children's academic success. She knew Sandra had been trying her best and she truly deserved a day such as this. Sandra was her only daughter and she couldn't wait to break the good news to her husband and the other family members, Sandra's two elder brothers.

Several times, Sandra have been made to know by some of their relative who would jokingly imply that women's education ends in the kitchen, Mama would always frown at that and would shun them whenever derogatory words are said to her daughter. Sandra would promise her to do her best in order to make her proud , and now, here she is, contemplating ongiving up every she once craved for, just because of something she never thought of, Love. It all started the day she was saved by Adex, and it wasn't his fault, she was the one who d ecided to pitch her tent with the devil.

It all began, two years ago on her first day in the university of Benin. The sun had retired to its abode and had passed on the duty to the moon and the stars, this wasn't their best day on duty as they could hardly illuminate the face of the earth. The evil ones always take delight in this, they love the moon, more that the sun because the sun wouldn't hide their evil deeds.

Sandra was dragged into an uncompleted building by the road side. 'Hey! If you really don't want to die, start removing your clothes off your body'. A young man with a coarse voice said to Sandra. She was stunned at the request of the man whose appearance resembled that of an assistant devil. The young man has on his body the tattoo of a dragon, his hair is dread locked and he was putting on a blue crazy jean.

Sandra was extremely scared as the evil man threatened to l aunch a broken bottle into her skin. She frets as his evil eyes feast on her delicate body. How she would escape her predator is what s he wasn't sure of. She prayed a silent prayer as she truly hoped that a savior would come. Just as if the great deity heard her prayer, her Savior arrived or should I say her saviors. The moon was bright enough to reveal the emergence of three other guys from the thick darkness.

'Sandra!' A voice called. She was jolted back to life by the pronunciation of her name. It was Ann, Sandra's childhood friend who had gained admission before her into the university of Benin. They had agreed tostay together in her hostel as she , Sandra wouldn't want to stay alone and since they knew each other so well, they agr eed to live together. She was traveling to school from Lagos, and she got to Benin City very late, as it was getting dark already, so she called Ann to inform her of her arrival, as she was walking through the street, she tried to trace Ann 's hostel as she had described to her earlier while they were chatting. As she was trying to find her way, these even men crossed her path and dragged her into an uncompleted building by the road side.

As the evil guys saw the approaching figures, they brought out their guns aiming it at the approaching figures. Ann, couldn't move further towards them and I could hear one of the b ad guys whispering to the others,'The wolf Lord.' Suddenly as if faced with great terror, they bolted away into the near bush, to Sandra's relief. Ann ran up to her and gave her a tight hug, after which she explained how she was coming from behind and could see when the bad guys dragged her into the uncompleted building with guns in their hands. "so, I decided to seek for help, as I was on my way back the hostel, I met these two brothers and plead with them to come for you r rescue." Ann explained.

Sandra looked towards the young men and couldn't identify their faces well because it was already dark, nevertheless, she needed to show gratitude to them. She walked up to them and said thank you to them. 'next time, be careful of walking in the night,' one of the guys finally sa id a word addressing her. "you might not be lucky next time', he added.

Sandra nodded in affirmation. She need not be preached to, she had learned her lessons obviously. They walked away from the uncompleted building and the two guys escorted them to Ann's hostel. After ensuring that they had got into their hostels, they turned back to leave. Just then, Sandra called them, 'Bross, what is your name?' 'Adex, call me Adex.' The first guy replied. "What about you?" Sandra asked facing the other guy. "don't worry about my name, the second guy replied her. "thank you once again. I owe you." Sandra said as the two guys, Adex and the unnamed guy walked away into the thick darkness.

Adex got into his apartment which wasn't void of people. The house is well furnished but untidy with bottles, cigarette and some other hard drugs. His entrance was greeted with shouts and hailing from t he guys who were busy with drinks and everything that can be smoked. "Capon!" they allsaluted. Adex saluted them as he entered the room. The other guys turned to greet the unnamed guy who just entered with Adex, 'how far Bullet?' one of the guys said, addressing the unnamed man. 'Guys, I experienced something strange and I am yet to comprehend it.' The guys all fixed their gaze on Bullet, apparently waiting for the gist from Bullet. Bullet explained how for the first time since he had been following Adex, he saved or helped someone. The report of Adex saving a random person seemed inconceivable to them. The guys in the room gave a look of astonishment. What they heard obviously sounded strange to them. 'what do you mean?' another guy asked. 'I said, today, the wolf rescued a lamb, isn't it unusual?' 'so unusual', they all chorused as they laughed nonstop.

Adekunle Bamgbopa was born into the family of a dreaded witch Hunter. As the first Child of his father, he had been exposed to a lot of metaphysical powers which made him so confident and fearless. His father had once shot him with a gun, with the bullet failing to penetrate into the delicate body of the young Adekunle. His father had empowered him w ith the famed *ayeta,* the mythical bullet proof he had even taken him on a journey into the wind, the *ofe* charm that would make one to disappear and appear in another place, the *oroka aluwo* was also in Dekunle's possession, a diabolical ring that makes one sprawl on the ground if beaten by it. Even though Baba Dekunle believed in metaphysical powers wholly, he had dreamt of Dekunle getting formal education and treading a more respectable life path to that which he had treaded and not just being feared alone.

Adekunle, just like his father became feared. His father had enrolled him into a primary school and no teacher would dare raise their cane to flog him, no matter what he does. He had the freedom of doing whatever he liked and no one would dare stop him, if the person still consider life w orth living. At a very young age, young guys would come to him to stay in his camp, at the age of twelve, he had become a don.

Adex got into the university and was soon recognized by the men of the underworld on campus. Winning Adex over to themselves by various cult groups was a highly contested i ncident, at last, Adex would pledge his allegiance to the wolves. Sooner than usual, he ascended the hierarchy of thefraternity and because of his fierceness, and unequal metaphysical prowess, he attained the position of the Capon, the Wolf Lord, after the previous wolf lord had been set up by a rival cult group and poisoned by a lady.

Adex reign would then strike fear into the heart of other cult group s and through his influence and reputation, the wolves became the strongest cult group on campus. Several conflict and fight will then surface, Adex would then flex his metaphysical powers, to the frustration of the other cult groups. But, just as every other powerful individual, there is always a way to bring them down and history should be believed, the greatest weakness of any man is Love. Adex knew this and would always rebuff any atom of love or feelings from himself. He wouldn't have a girlfriend rather, he would rather have casual sex without any emotional attachment. He believed, that abstaining from women would protect him from the greatest threat to his powers and invisibility, Love .

On the day Sandra was almost raped. Adex was returning back home from the joint where he had taken some strong drinks, he had never walked alone, the wolf lord never should. That explains why he was with Bullet. When Ann rushed to him, surprisingly, the devil in him refused to surface, to the surprise of Bullets, who watch on as Adex told Ann to take him to the place where her friend was taken to. Bullet, followed in disbelief. This was the first time Adex would answer a call for help. In fact, many times, people are too scared to get close to him because he walks with fire in his eyes. He never laughed and he is a man of very few words, most often than not, he is always quiet which made him very much unpredictable. Whatever had made Adex give attention to something that is not war must be a mystery. Bullet could only hope that the fierce wolf is not starting to develop a soft spot which would be a clear weakness.

CHAPTER TWO

BEAUTY AND THE BEASTS

'Hey! Sleeping beauty. Welcome to the university of Benin. I hope you will learn your lesson that, here, one of the constitution or commandments is thou shall not walk alone in the night if at all thou shall walk in the night at all.' Sandra tries to open her eyes as she saw Ann with a sarcastic face. She hissed and pulled the blanket on herself. 'You had better get up, you obviously are lagging behind with your registration'. Sandra jumped off the bed as she heard Ann's last statement. She ought to have been around earlier for the registration. She quickly ran into the bathroom to have her shower after which she dressed up and ate the breakfast that Ann had already prepared.

After returning from the school, Ann, who

happened to be in her third year in the school welcomed Sandra back home. 'you didn't go to school, do you?' Sandra asked, as she was surprised to leave Ann at home and still meether at home. It's the first week of resumption my dear, nothing much happens during the first weeks. How is the registration going?' Ann asked Sandra, who is busy taking off her clothes. 'my dear, stressful is an understatement. Honestly, I am exhausted.' 'welcome to University of Calabar once again', Ann said, laughing at Sandra. 'I know that you will be tired and famished, so, I have made something delicious for you to eat, just go into the bathroom, take a shower and comeback to eat the delicacy that I have prepared for you. 'Thanks sweetheart, you are the best!' Sandra said as she wrapped her towel on her body and disappear into the bathroom.

'You are a great cook Ann. " Sandra made a comment after her first bite of the food. "Yes, I know.' Ann said proudly and they both chuckled. As they were eating Sandra reflected on the incident that happened the previous day. She wondered why it took less than twenty-four hours to have such a horrible experience. She has heard about the rugged life in the historical citadel of learning and it was an unpleasant surprise to have that experience that early. She was brought back to life by Ann, who had been talking to her believing that she was hearing what she had be saying only to discover that her mind had travelled far away to ano ther land. 'Hey! Girlfriend, what sup, you seem to be lost.' Ann reacted to Sandra's absent mindedness. 'I am sorry, I never knew I had gone that far.' Sandra apologized. Ann wouldn't let the conversation slide, so, he went further to ask what she was thinking. 'Do you know those guys that rescued us yesterday?' Sandra asked. Ann gave her a quizzical look and wondered why on earth Sandra was asking about the guys.

As far as she knows, they are some influential guys in the rugged land of Benin. 'I don't know much about the guys, just like I told you, a Course mate of me referred me to them.' Ann explained. 'I heard one of the bad guys whisper a name to the others, I guess that name struck fear into the bad guys before they fled.' Ann's face lightened up, she adjusted her sitting position and encouraged Sandra to continue with what she was say ing. 'What is the name that you heard, she asked curiously. 'I heard the guy whisper the wolf.' Like the sound of a thunder, Ann was struck with great fear. She had hear d that name several times, but she doesn't and would never had imagined speaking to the person who bears the name that strike fear into the whole of the great university of Benin.

Sandra noticed how terrified Ann was and asked her why she panickedwhen she mentioned the name. 'Sandra, you were rescued by the devilhimself.' Sandra couldn't understand what Ann meant. 'The devil?' Annwouldn't speak further. "Do not ever get close to him again If you so much love your dear life ." Ann warned. All Sandra could do is to stare at Ann, as she couldn't understand the magnitude of the fear on her face. Even though Adex is tagged as 'the devil' she still owes her some appreciation, at least, thedevil rescued her.

After the lecture, one a Friday afternoon, Sandra was rushing home from school as she was already starving as she couldn't eat before leaving for school that morning, as she was rushing out, she ran into a group of guys, mistakenly stepping on one of the guy's toes unaware. The closer guy to her dragged her back. 'hey! are you blind?' Sandra was not sure what she had done to provoke the guy into asking her that kind of offensive question. As she was about to fire back at the guy who she believed had accused her wrongly only to look up to see the devil who once rescued her in the past coming right behind the guys. She snatched off her hand from the guy who held her hand and ran to Adex. 'Finally, I meet you again.' She said with a glowing smile on her face. 'thanks for the other day.' Sandra said, looking at the seemingly confused Adex. 'hey! Move back!' Bullet casted a dreadful look at Sandra. 'sorry, I don't know you.' Adex said still looking at her as if he was trying to remember something. Adex looks a little calmer and nice than everyone opined of him, at least, that was Sandra's opinion. 'I am the lady you saved from being raped the other day, I hope that you remember me now?' she said with a smile on her face.

Now, Adex could remember her face. 'it's okay, I think I can rememberyou now. It's okay. ' He took the step to leave walking away from her. Sandra turned back and walk up to him again. 'hey! You are the wolf lord, aren't you?' all the guys around, turned to Sandra with great fury. 'and who the hellare you?' one of the guys barked at Sandra. 'shhh! I wasn't talking to you.' Sandra used her hand to hold her lips, signaling him to keep his mouth shut. All the guys were stunned. They couldn't imagine any one daring to look into the face or challenge any member of the w olves.

Stone, one of the guys charged towards Sandra and tried to hit her on her face. Adex raised his hand signaling Stone to hold back and he gave a hysteric laugh. He was surprised and thrilled to see someone finally standing up against him. A woman for that matter. 'yes, I am the wolf lord. Now that you know, what can I do for you'. 'Your name sparks fear in the heart of all and sundry. I even heard that you are like a devil, the one who fights fearlessly and without mercy.' So, I was wondering, if you are really that dangerous, why did you help me?' Adex, chuckled with a wicked smile on his face. 'you wouldn't want me to answer your question on the road side, next time, when our path crosses, ask your questions and I would answer you. He turned away and moved away with his company.   Sandra had forgotten that she was hungry, she quickly, turned back to her way home with anticipation of meeting the dreaded Adex again.

Sandra decided to gist her friend Ann, about her encounter with Ad exwhile she was on her way back home. Ann stared in disbelief that Sandra would take such dangerous boldness. 'Sandra, I have warned you several times, I hope this your foolish boldness will not lead to your downfall very soon.' Nothing will happen to me, she said nonchalantly.

Adex pondered on the incident that happened the previous day. He was wondering about the kind of boldness exhibited by Sandra. It occurred to him he didn't even get to know her name. somehow, he was feeling calm with her. Usually, no one would have dared to look at him in the face. He kept on imagining the scenario over and over again. He let out a sly smile as he recalled the face of Stone when, Sandra told him to shut up. For a very long time, Adex didn't know when he began to smile.

CHAPTER THREE

A NEW FRIEND

School work began to get more demanding. Several individual and group assignments were piling up for her. Even though she was enjoying school, sometimes, the stress can be discouraging. Sandra wasn't one of the brightest students in the department but she is determined to do just enough not to fail. Sandra decided to make friends that would be of help to her academically. Since it was the first semester in school, she could only assume the brilliant once in the class based on their active participation during lectures and she decided to befriend Esther. One of those who seemed to be brighter in the class . It turned out to be a great decision as herperformance improved greatly. Life in school was going on greatly with a lot of escapades, and she was ready to enjoy every bit of it.

Many days passed by, days turned int o weeks and weeks into months. Adex and Sandra's path never crossed until destiny brought them together once more. Esther, Sandra's friend invited her over to her apartment, to work on an assignment together. On their way to her house, they walked past a guy who was putting on a yellow shirt with a blue trouser. 'hey! Estherthe voice called.' Esther had wanted to avoid him, but they had a lready run into him. 'Hello, Collins.' Esther greeted him casually. 'you have obviously been avoiding me.' C ollins had been after Esther since she stepped into the school and nothing, she would do would make him stop pestering her.

Sandra took some steps further away from them to give them space for their dialogue. Esther would make him realize that she isn't interested in any relationship, at least not in her early days in the university. She believed that it would be a high distraction to her.

While Sandra was waiting for Esther, she could sight Bullet coming out of a corner. She has not been able to find out what her name was. Immediately Bullet saw Sandra, his countenance changed as if he had seen a bad omen. Just as he was trying to manage himself and walk past her, he saw Collins and Esther. He and Collins exchange bitter looks. I t was like two sworn enemies met. The two guys smirked at each other as Bullet bounced off. 'Who is that guy and why did you guys react to each other in such manner.' Collins wouldn't answer the question as he just waved the scenario as it's nothing serious.

Collins pleaded with Esther to at least give him

her number. After so much persuasion. She gave Collins her phone number. 'I will flash you with mine, please, ensured that you save the number.' he said this, giving Esther some cute smile. 'it's alright.' Esther replied as she walked back towards Sandra who had been waiting for s ome minutes now.

Sandra was curious about Collins and what he had to do with Bullet ormaybe the wolves. She asked Esther about who Collins is. Esther couldn't supply enough information about him as he was just getting to know him. 'Why do you ask.' Esther said, directing the question to Sandra. Sandra told her that she was just curious, refusing to disclose to her that she k new the other guy to be one of the famous cult group on Campus. That is the wolves.

The following week, Sandra decided to go with the library to read. Shehad been severally invited to the library by Esther who obviously was a very studious student. She walked into the library building which was greeted with great tranquility. The hole building was filled up with students which made Sandra to question her seriousness.

This was the first time she will be coming into the school library, she was walking inside the library, trying to secure a space for herself in the overcrowded room. Luckily for her a young lady stood up from a seat as she was about to leave the room. Sandra quickly secured the seat for herself. After settling down, she rose to get some textbooks from the book shelve. After she returned, she noticed that the person sitting right there beside him was Collins, the guy Esther was talking to the other day. The guy who exchanged a strange look with Bullet. She wondered why someone who is associated with Bullet, whether friends or foes should also be seen in a place such as the library. She thought of standing up from the seat and find another space for herself but she might not find another space soon. 'Hey! Sandy, focus on the reason why you a re here.' She said to herself. So, she brought out her jotter as she began to write down the things that she read from the textbooks she had picked up from the book shelve previously.

After a while, Collins packed his bag and was about to leave, just then, she sighted Sandra, he paused for a while trying to recall the face and finally, he did. 'hey! You were with Esther the other day, aren't you?' Sandra had been praying that Collins leaves the room without noticing her, she wasn't in the mood to engage in a conversation at the moment. So, she just nodded in affirmation without taking her face away from her book. 'I am Collins.'

The guy introduced. Collins have this kind of accent that is American. Hiswell shaved hair and neatly ironed shirt with his calmness defies the reputation of being a bad guy. Sandra would wait till like forever before she could reply Collins. 'Collins, it's okay. It's nice to know.' 'wouldn't you tell me yours?' Collins asked a little bit taken aback by Sandra's reaction. 'is that really necessary?' Sandra said to herself. She felt that something even might end up happening getting close to this guy. But at last, she decided to be a little nice with him, since he had always proved to be a gentle man. 'my name is Sandra.' She eventually

revealed. 'Sandra what?' Collins askedfurther. Sandra became a little bit impatient with Collins and couldn't help being a little bit rude to him this time around. 'Collins, the last time I checked, this is a library and not a party or date where you have all freedomto discuss unnecessary topics.'Collins   got offended with

Sandra's words. He wanted to tell her that she lacks manner, but that wouldn't be a nice thing to say to a friend of someone he hopes to win her heart, so he gently apologized. 'I am sorry, I must have met you in the wrongmood.' Collins said as he walked out of the library.

'Did he just apologize?' Sandra asked herself in utter disbelief. 'wow! He must definitely be a perfect gentle man.' But where and how could he have known bullet remains something to ponder on by Sandra.

After some hours in the library, Sandra was pleased with herself, she had really been able to find answers to many questions she did not understand well. She decided in her heart that she would form the habit o f coming to the library more often than ever before. She packed her bag and went back home. She had stopped discussing anything about Adex or anything that has to do with the wolves.

Bullet walked up to Adex, who was sitting under a tree with some roll of marijuana in his hand and a bottle of alcohol. 'boss!' Bullet hailed. Adex didn't reply as he was busy with the stuff in his hand. Adex decided to tell him about seeing Sandra and Collins. 'Adex, I saw that babe today.' Thatdidn't seem to have any effect on his attention as he was still acting as if noone was talking to him. Bullet decided to continue anyway. 'I saw the babe that you helped, the babe that told us to shut up and ask if you are truly the wolf lord.' Now, Adex turned to him and gave his si gnatory smile, the devil'ssmile. 'Bullet, what about the girl this time, what as she done again?' 'boss,you have never been soft with anyone like this before, Boss! I don't know,but I feel this girl is a bad omen and should be taken far away from you.' Adex gave his smile again, this time, he exaggerated his laughter. 'Bullet, thereason why the lion is the king of the jungle is because the Lion is never fazed by any other animal in the jungle. That girl is too small of a threat to me, so let her be.' He let out his laughter again. 'Boss! I saw her few days agowith the striker of the blades.' Adex eyes lightened up when he heard Bullet's last word. 'The blade's striker? The deadliest weapon of the Blades.' Bullet was glad that finally, he is making sense to Adex. Suddenly Adex letout a laughter again. 'No matter what, the lion remains the king of thejungle.' He laughed again. Bullet left him as he entered into the large room, Adex apartment.

Collins continued to seek ways to win Esther's heart but alw ays get very uncomfortable each time Sandra gets into the picture. He would want to strangle her to death sometimes. He detests her obvious arrogance. But one thing he could not hate about her is her obvious courage and fearlessness. He had met very few people who can be as daring as Sandra is and that alone made him have some soft spot for her. Somewhere deep within his heart, he has a liking for her. There rose a battle in him and he never wish or wanted to love her. The thought of her arrogance should be enough to strangle any form of affection that he can possibly have for her, hopefully, so he thought but the more he gets closer to Esther and encountering Sandra, the more he began to develop admiration for her, coupled with the fact that, no one has ever pay very little or no attention to him before just as she had always done. There seemed to be a hurricane coming, one even the king of the jungle isn't ready for.

CHAPTER FOUR

LOVE FROM A DISTANCE

The first semester ran to an end and most students went back to theirvarious homes. Sandra, returned back to Lagos. It was a relieving period away from the school stress. Mr and Mrs Badejo, were glad to welcome their beautiful daughter back home. Mr Badejo is a successful business man witha lot of wealth and properties. Sandra was the only female child of the family.The family status of Sandra's family was one of the reasons why she can sometimes act arrogantly. Sandra's two brothers who are also older than her had always protected her, one of the reasons why she always had the gut to look into the eyes of any guy. The holiday seemed so short to Sandra. She wished to spend more time with her family at home, so she did not resume when others did.

After eventually returning to school, she had missed some classes and several notes. She quickly reached out to Esther and requested for notes from her. She decided to visited her so that she can explain the notes to her. During the weekend, Sandra went to Esther's house. On getting to the house,he met a male footwear at the door post. She knocked the door and Esthercame to open the door to her. 'Sandra, what sup? You didn't tell me that you will be coming around.' 'Sorry I didn't call to inform you, can I come inside?' Esther who had forgotten that she was standi ng at the door, hinderingSandra from coming inside suddenly realized that. 'oh! I am sorry, please come inside.' Sandra entered and the person who own the shoe outside was Collins, he was seating on Esther's bed. Sandra wasn't expecting to see him, even though she felt that she had always been unfair to him, in the way that she treats him, yet, she takes joy in making the poor young man uncomfortable. 'hello Sandy.' Collins greeted with a cute smile on his face. 'Hi.' Sandra replied as casual as always.

'Esther, I might have to come back, since you ha ve a guest here. I came for the explanation to the notes I missed but, you are obviously not free at the moment, so I will have to come back.' 'You can't go back because of me, don't worry, I promise not to d isturb your study.' Collins said, still maintaining the smile on his face. 'Sandra, don't worry, Collins won't be a disturbance.' Sandra decided to stay.

Esther brought out her own note as she began to explain to her. Whenthey got to a particular topic, Esther couldn't explain neither does she understand the topic, it was on calculation. After some minutes that they had been sweating on the topic, for the first time since they have started studying, Collins spoke. 'Can I help you guys with it.' just as if she had been waiting for it, Esther replied 'sur e if you can.' Sandra, couldn't help but imagine if Collins would not be able to tackle the problem, she would definitely mock him. She, patiently waited for Collins to f umble but to her surprise and to the amazement of Esther herself, Collins explained the topic in details, Sandra couldn't believe how brilliant Collins was and for the first time, Collins find a way to win her respect. He had explained better than Esther would. Of course, that is expected of a three hundred level Statistics student.

After the tutorial, Sandra appreciated Collins. 'Thanks for the help, Collins. I do appreciate.' Collins was surprised to hear that from Sandra. She had never been polite at least based on his own judgment and evaluation.

He was glad that his intelligence could earn him some respect from someone like Sandra. Sandra could be anything but definitely not an ingrate. She had learned that from her mother who will always encourage them to show gratitude whenever they are shown any act of kindness or benevolence. 'Wow! Did you just say Thank you?' Collins couldn't resist the temptation of showing his surprise. Sandra smiled. 'I don't know you can be as intelligent as this. Maybe I should show you some more respect.' Collins was actually proud of himself at this point and Esther was also glad that finally, Sandra is beginning to treat Collins whom she had begun to fall in love with nicely.

Collins begin to get along well with Sandra and so on, the three of them became inseparable from one another. The closer they get the more Collins develops strong feelings for Sandra, something he would never have imagined. Sandra on the other hand innocently related to Collins as just a mere friend. Of course, she wouldn't consider betraying her friend Estherwho had become overly in love with Collins, Collins played along but his heart now delights in the one who never appeal to him.

Soon, Esther would tell Sandra to go with her to Collins hostel whenever there is a topic that they needed more explanations about. Sandra and Collins had formed a great friendship with Esther that Sandra wouldn't see it as any crime to study in Collins apartment. Soon the wild fire of love begins to burn in Collins heart that she struggled to conceal his feelings for Sandra. Many thoughts would run through his mind each time he thinks about telling Sandra about how he feels. He was afraid of losing Esther's friendship, he was also scared of Sandra rejecting his feelings so he chose thesafer option, which is keeping his feelings to himself.

CHAPTER FIVE

THE DEVIL'S HEART

Adex couldn't get rid of the girl who dared to talk to him without any iota of fear. Something in him desired to see her again despite the warning from Bullet that the girl is likely going to bring evil or bad luck upon Adex himself. Adex wondered what the girl could possibly have to do with Collins,he wondered if her relationship with Collins was what gave her that kind of boldness. He had sent one of his guys and to investigate Sandra. He was later informed that Collins is only dating Sandra's friend and not Sandra herself.

'Did, the poor girl know that she is dating Death's deadliest weapon.' Adex said to himself. 'I just hope that the poor lady doe s.' he let out that laughter once more. 'Collins, the g reen snake under the green grass, the biggest havoc with the most enticing smile, only if the girl knows.'

Few weeks later, Sandra had gone to the school cafeteria to eat with Esther, Collins had promised to catch up with them there, so they had to wait for him. After a while, Sandra ordered for a plate of rice, she couldn't wait any more since she was starving. Esther decided to wait till Collins arrives before she could order for whatever she wanted to order. S andra was served with the plate of rice and a big lap of chicken. She also requested for achilled Fanta drink, that was her favorite. She began to feast on the enticing and palatable food before her.

Not too long after she had started eating, suddenly the other studentsinside the cafeteria began to stand up and were leaving with fear written allover their faces, many of them without even finishing the food they wereeating. Esther got scared as she tapped Sandra who was just focus on the food before her. 'Sandra, let's go.' Esther whispered. She ha d noticed that theexodus from the cafeteria was preceded by the entrance of some men in black attire, she could recognize Bullet as the one who gave Collins an unfriendly look the other day they me t. Their outlook looks scary and at thecenter of these men was a man who dressed a little bit different from theothers. He was putting on a red cloth with black trousers. Sandra, wasn'tsure of the reason why Esther would suddenly ask them to leave whenobviously Collins who had promised to join them had not arrived. It thensuddenly dawns on her that everyone in the cafeteria had left, this broughther consciousness to the guys whose presence instigated the exodus. 'It's thewolves.' Sandra said to herse lf. 'Sandra, I said let's go.' Esthershouted at her out of fear but Sandra did not flinch. Esther stood up andmoved towards the exit but was stopped by Bullet, who stood on herway. 'Esther Aderibigbe.' he called out Esther's name and Surname. Estherwas so shocked, what could she have done to be known my me n like this,she wondered. 'I am just wondering if you know who the man you are datingreally is, you don't seem to know, if you do, you will not be this Coward.' Bullet said as he gave a wicked smil e before making way for her to pass.After which one of the guys went to the waiter and deliver an instruction to her.

After Sandra had finished her food, she stood up and moved towards the exit of the cafeteria. Just then, she turned back and walked towa rds Adexwho had been watching her since they entered the cafeteria. She walked upstraight to him and drew out a chair and sat. 'Must you come to a place like this when you know that your presence will scare people off, you could have chosen another place to it if you must eat outside your home.' Sandra'swords infuriated the men in black but surprisingly, it thrills Adex himselfwho smiled. 'this is question number three.' Adex said to her stillmaintaining the smile on his face. 'asking questions must be your hobby.' he said again jokingly.

Sandra sternly looked into Adex's eyes and said, 'Adex, even though you are the Wolf Lord, you have a heart and deep inside every heart, there is what makes him human. And the blessing of being a human is the beauty oflove, affection and compassion towards one another, without wish a man's life is in mystery.' These words struck Adex's heart.

He pondered on each word for a while to really digest and understand it. The other guys in black had settled on other seats in the cafeteria giving space to Adex and Sandra. Finally, the seemingly emotionless Adex feltremorseful, at least that was what Sandra thought. Only for him to burst into laughter again. 'Power! Power is the most beautiful thing in life my dear.It makes people give you the respect that you deserve and gives you the unlimited access to freedom. Being human is a weakness to maintainingpower. That is why we refuse to cower like everyone who left when we arrived, it creates space for us, that is what power ca n get you.' for the firsttime, Adex, seems to be willing to engage in a proper conversation, something that thrills Sandra. She thought for a while to back up her points. 'You are right, Power is great, but when it is wrongly used,its

beings fear and not love and respect. While when power if rightly used can turn a man into a hero, one who isn't feared but re spected andloved, one who will truly enjoy the beauty of life and the warmth embrace of live of the people around him. This is one with the great est power, love.'Sandra's words seemed to always have effect on Adex, who was really touched by the words of Sandra. She seemed so smart coupled with hercourage, she began to melt Adex's heart away, melt all the rearguard he has about loving. 'What is your name again?' Adex asked staring into Sandra'seyes. 'Finally, the mighty Adex cares to know my name. I guess he s till has aheart.' Sandra said with a smile on her face. Adex too was forced to smile. 'That is it,' Sandra thought, deep inside him, there is a kind, lovely andlikeable individuals. 'Sandra is my name. And it is nice to meet a very little part of this real you.' Adex smiled again.

After the discussion, Sandra picked up her bag and was about to leave. 'Sandra, drop your contact here, I would love to talk to you again.' Adex said, stretching his phone towards Sandra who paused for a while before obliging to his request after which she left. Adex was impressed with her audacity. He wondered where she could have gotten her courage from, unconscio usly he had begun to fall in love with Sandra even though he would never want to admit it.

Adex couldn't get Sandra off his mind, every moment he spent with her made him look so different, different from what he had always felt with other people. So, he decided to see Sandra again, he dialed Sandra's number and after the phone rang for a while Sandra responded. 'Hello! Who is this.' she enquired? She wasn't expecting Adex's call, he sounds so calm yet assertive on the phone. 'I want to see you today.' he sa id. Sandra laughedand asked him to ask to see her like a gentleman and not like the Wolf Lord.Adex chuckled. 'Okay Madame Sandra, can we meet each other today.' Sandra thought for a while and decided to oblige. Who knows, she could be able to take the devil and make several people study in peace on campuswhen the devil is tamed but she gave him a condition, she would only agree to meet with him only if he is not accompanied by his disciples. After he hadbeen silent for a while, Adex consented to the con dition. He promised tosend the location where they will be meeting to her by 6pm that evening.

Adex dressed up, he wore a well ironed T-Shirt and black trousers. He reached out to his collection of perfumes and wore the *Night Walker* on himself. That was his favorite. He reached out to his black well-polished shoe as he slides it into his feet. He put on his wrist watch and chains.

Coming out of his room, he was met with gazes that were full of disbelief. This was the first time Adex would dress like this. Bullet and stone jumped up immediately. They were al l too stunned to pass a remark concerning Adex dress. Adex noticed that Bullet and Stone had gotten up, trying to follow him as they had always done, but this time, he restricted them. The guys all seemed confused but none of them could question Adex.

Just as he was about to leave, Bullet raised his voice. 'It is about that girl, isn't it?' Adex stopped after Bullet's words. He turned back to see the burning eyes of Bullet. Adex decided not to give any r esponse to him and he continued his movement towards the door. 'Don't you dare walk out on us without an explanation of where you are going to and why we shouldn't be in your company.' the whole room was in grave silence. Everyone was shocked to see that for the first time ever, one person stood up to qu estion and have the audacity to dare Adex among the wolves. Adex turned back in anger, he looked into Bullet's face. 'I am still Adex, Adekunle Bangbopa, the Wolf Lord, never don't forget that an old Lion is still no match for the dig.' he banged up the door and left.

Sandra slide into a blue gown, she put on her wig and waited for Ann, her roommate to return so that she can tell her about going out. Not too long after then, Ann entered. Seeing Sandra dressed up already, she coulddecide that she's on her way out. 'So, where is my darling friend heading toat this time of the day.' she asked with a mischievous smile on her face.Sandra wouldn't dare tell her that she was going to see Adex. She is very much aware that Ann would do anything to stop her if she gets to know. Ifthere is anyone who could really stand on her way from doing what she has decided to do, then Ann should be the person. She only told her that she would be going to see a friend. Ann pretended to be choked as she let out aprolong coughs. She would go ahe ad to tease her, 'my regards to him please.'Sandra, was forced to let out a smile. 'and who told you that the friend is a he?' They both burst into laughter, Sandra said her good bye and exi ted theroom.

Sandra and Adex met at one of the luxurious eateries in town. Sandra was some minutes late, while she entered the eatery, she tried to locate Adexwho had called earlier to inform her that he had gotten to the venue. She then saw a young man waving at her. She couldn't recognize quickly that it was Adex. He looked so different this time around. She walked up to where he seated and sat facing him. They both ordered for something to eat as they begin to discuss, the more they chatted, the more A dex gets deeper in his love for her. For a very long time, someone t reats him like every other person are treated. He didn't know when he laughed to the extent that he forgot that, he is Adex, the Wolf Lord. 'Adek unle Bangbopa, I like this version of you.' Sandra said as she watched Adex's smile. She noticed that Adex was good looking after all and he is such a good listener. They had a swell time together after which they decided to take a walk. As they were going, Adex held Sandra's hand. They continued chatting and laughing, just then, Adex, stopped and stared into Sandra's eyes.

'Sandra, I think that I am in love with you, I love you Sandra.' Sandra was caught unprepared for this confession. 'You make me feel different and I love what I feel about me rig ht now. If having you in my life would make this feeling remain, then, I would love to spend my forever with you .' Sandra was left speechless, she wanted to say a word but her lips seemed heavy to move. She had begun to like Adex but it wasn't anything romantic. Many thought floods her mind, he had finally played with the devil's heart, she was lost in thought when Adex planted a kiss on her lips. When she finally gained consciousness, she raised her head in disbelief that Adex had actually kissed her, then she saw Collins standing right behind Adex with a teary eye, he turned back immediately and walk away swiftly.

Sandra quickly dispatched herself from Adex arm and she ran back to her hostel, leaving Adex glued to the spot with no comprehension of why Sandra had run away. Adex walked slowly and sadly on the road side, he hadnever imagined that something like this would ever happen to him. Love seemed to be a force that is stronger, much stronger than human will . The thought of Sandra not loving him in re turn made him extremely week, he was ready to do anything now just to ensure that he wins her he art.

Sandra got back home in a different mood to the one he came with. Ann was disturbed about the sudden change in her mood. She couldn't understand how Adex had quickly fallen in love with her and also the reasonfor the tears in Collins face. She wished she had not said yes to Adex's invitation earlier. She wouldn't say anything to Ann who trie d her best to make her talk. In fact, she couldn't eat the food that Ann had prepared for her. Just within few hours everything took a new turn with her. Hmm, love definitely is no respecter of anybody, it happens to anyone, rich and poor, young and old, now, even the devil 's heart can be taken by love .

After the incidence, Collins wouldn't show up at Esther's place, and hewould always make excuse of not been at home each time Esther ask to come over to his place, Sandra too wouldn't talk to Esther as before, she suddenly became a different person entirely, a different p erson to the usually confident young lady who had floored Adex heart.

CHAPTER SIX

CONFESSION

Sandra would no longer pick Adex calls and has never seen or walk into Collins. Esther, decided to go to her family during the weekend to visit her Mum who was reportedly rushed to the hospital. She was at home when she received a call from Jay boy, Collins only friend that she knows. Jayboy informed her that Collins was very sick and had refused to go to the hospital, Esther was so bothrered, she wondered what could have gone wrong with him. She thanked Jayboy for reaching out to him and after ending the call, she put a call through to Sandra. She informed Sandra of Collins ailment and made Sandra promise to go and pay him a visi t.

Sandra went to Collins house the f ollowing morning. She knocked the door to his apartment and a young fair skinned lady in her night wear opened the door. 'hello, good morning.' The lady greeted. Sandra wondered who the girl was. This was the first time she will be seeing her. 'goodmorning.' Sandra said in return. 'pl ease is Collins in?' Sandra asked politely. 'yes, he is, though he is indisposed at the moment. 'if you don't mind, can I see him. 'sure, you can come inside.' The lady said as she opened the doorfor Sandra to come in. She led Sandra to the room where Col lins was laying.

Collins had gotten so lean as he had refused to eat consistently. Tears almost dropped at her eyes seeing his condition. The fair lady turned to leave the two of them behind in the room. Just as she was abou t to get out of

the door, Collins called her back 'Mary, meet Sandra.' Sandra then turned to Sandra and stared into her eyes which made Sandra uncomfortable. 'Oh, it's

nice to finally meet you Miss Sandra, Collins had said a lot about you.' She stretched her hand to shake Sandra. 'my na me is Mary, Collins only sibling.' She finally introduced. Sandra stretch her hand to have the handshake with her. 'It's nice meeting you too Mary, Collins never mentioned having a sister.' Sandra said, casting a glance at Co llins who is still on the bed. 'that is because you never asked.' Collins defended himself. The three of them laughed and Mary excused herself from them.

'Do you love him?' Collins asked immediately Mary left the room. Sandra pretended not to hear what he had said and Collins repeated his question. Sandra couldn't understand why all that Collins could be concern about at that point is if she loved Adex. 'Collins, I really can't answer that question. Moreover, you should do your best to recover from your sic knesson time. 'Sandra, I don't know how to say this, before, I never thought a time will come when something like this would happen but, that moment that Isay him kissing you, I felt like my heart is being ripped off, I never told you how I felt because I was scared that I might lose your friendship and that ofyour friend Esther. Since the day, you came to Esther's house to study, my heart had been yawning to love you. I am sick because I couldn't bear thethought of losing you. Sandra, please, don't break my heart.' More than before. Sandra got more confused.

Mary entered, it was like she had been standing at the door eavesdropping on their conversation. She knelt and began to plead with Sandra to accept her brother . 'This is the first time I am seeing him in this state, please don't make his life miserable.' Sandra, was left speechless, no word would come out of her mouth. Esther had been a wonderful friend to her, it would be a betrayal of the highest order to com e in-between her and the man she loved. She told Collins that she wou ld think about it, being careful not to aggravate his ill health. She left Collins house more confused than ever before, and she knew that if she wasn't careful, her result would

suffer, so she resulted to avoiding them all, the library would be a good place to take solace, since Collins don't visit there often and Adex's shadow has never been seen anywhere close to the library.

Esther returned from home and paid Collins a visit , she got some some provisions for him and would spend time with him after school.

Soon, Collins began to return to his usual self, and Esther was really glad about it.

CHAPTER SEVEN

THE MUTE POOR GENIUS

Sandra would often resume at the library immediately after lectures and wouldn't leave till dusk. Soon, she began to get obsessed with learning, an incident that reflected in her grades. Esther noticed that she had refrained from her and she doesn't visit her as often as she used to, Sandra would always use studying as a noble excuse to explai n why she had not been coming around. During her frequent visit to the library, she noticed one of her course mates, Olusegun Samuel.

Samuel had never been seen talking to anyone before. He had alwaysbeen so quiet and reserved. Every time Sandra goes to the library, she always meets him there and she would always leave him there. She wondered if the guy ever goes home. After a week of her new-found love with the library, she had been preparing for a test, as much as she had studied, she still finds itdifficult to solve some problems, she thoughts going to Esther, but the thought of meeting Collins in her place made her shelf the idea. Suddenly, it occurred to her that the quiet student might be of help. 'Hello! She said after walking up to him.' she sat beside him and noticed that the young mandidn't respond to her greeting, 'maybe he didn't hear her the first time he said to herself as she greeted again but to her surprise, she got no responsewhatsoever, this made her get mad as she pulled away the note in front of the guy who had his face fixed to the spot where the note was.

'Who are you that you are so full of yourself?'
Sandra barked at him in anger, drawing the
attention of the people in the library to her side,
'hello,please you can't make noise like this here,
this is a library', the librariancautioned. Sandra felt
embarrassed, she wishes that she could strangle his
neck, she packed her books as she set to leave on
anger onl y to be withheldby the guy himself. He
held her and for the first time she heard him speak.
'Sorry, I am sorry.' Sandra paused and wanted to be
sure that it was the guy who actually spoke, her
heart melted immediately as she sat down. 'now,
how can I help you.' the voice as ked calmly. 'My
name is Olusegun, I don'tneed to ask about yours
because I know that you are Sandra, the daring one.'
Sandra could not understand what he meant, but
she would find that outlater, presently, the only
thing that she's concerned about is her test. 'Can
you help me with the explanation to this?' she asked
politely as she showedSegun her note.

Sandra was left dumbfounded, he seemed to even know the topic more than the teacher who taught them. 'you must be one of the best students in our department.' she remarked. Segun smiled and told her to find that out herself. Sandra could see his matriculation number on one of his textbooks and she planned to check out for his grade when she gets home as she still has the picture of the previous semester results that was pasted on her phone.

After the study, she thanked Segun who apologized for his previous action. Sandra went back home satisfied and ready for the test. She was glad that she didn't allow her anger to hinder what she had gained from him. She felt that she had also been guilty of what she had gotten mad at Segun for, her reaction towards Collins crossed her mind. She smiled as she had learnt to be nice to people having been on the receiving end of not being treated nicely.

Sandra later discovered that Segun had the highest grade in her department, and no one gets close to his grade mark. She wondered if being quiet is a secret to becoming extremely brilliant and she began to spend more time with him in the library, she was the only friend Seg un had, but she has this feeling, there is so much about this quiet genius she hasn't figured out yet and as fate would have it, she began to grow fond of him without even noticing it.

CHAPTER EIGHT

THE CHOICE OF LOVE

Esther had noticed Collins coldness towards her. This obviously wasn'tthe Collins who was head and toe in love with her. Life had thought her so many lessons, she never wanted to start this because she had once experienced the brutal side of love towards those who are enslaved by it. Esther confronted Collins, who ended up saying that he no longer has feelings for her. It was as if her heart was r ipped off her chest, though it had been a awhile, she called Sandra, who rushed over to her place after hearing her bitter voice on the phone.

Esther broke the news to Sandra, Collins is gone, far away from her reach, he had now loved another woman. Sandra was quiet as she drew her close and hugged her. Esther, would then narrate why it took her so long to accept the love offer proposed to her by Collins. she recounted:

'While growing up, life was nothing but perfect. I mean, perfect! My

Sister and I had everything we wanted. It was just the both of us or so I thought. Mom, Dad, there's this guy that'd come around occasionally, Dayo, I used to refer to him as my cousin. He 's 13 years older than I am. I was the first child, that's what I made myself believe. And then, there's Anu, my sister, a light complexioned girl. She's four years my junior. I and of course, myself.

Father wasn't employed but mother was. Her work was paying reallywell so we didn't have no worry. She is a Nurse, a senior one and she was working in one of the biggest hospitals in town. She was pretty close to the man who owns the hospital, so she was like the second in command; Jeezlife was good. So, so good. You wouldn't know father is not employed if youare not told. Everything was going on fine at home. Mother bought most of the properties in his name: land, cars and almost all that we had.

We attended the best private school in town. Mother would pay ou rfees before the school would even ask us to pay. Then, the bus allowance -that's for people that the school bus would carry to and from school, it's supposed to be paid monthly but Mother would pay for like a year eventhough I rarely go with the school bus, there was a driver whose only job is to always drop my sis and I in school daily, he'd come pick us when school closes as well.

The reason mother paid that fee is to establish a plan B in casethe driver wouldn't be available, but he was. Always.

Pupils in my school would get sent out when they don't pay the schoolfees. And I'd always long to be amongst them just so I'd have the luxury to roam the street and feel like one of them. I didn't understand why their parents won't pay their fees. Another thing that bugs me is why some children in my class would always bring Yam porridge, constantly. Is it that they are so in love with just that one meal? Or... I just couldn't figure it out. You can't blame me: I thought life was as good as it was in my place , everywhere else. Later, I had a reason to understand why things were that way.

Mother took care of all her siblings. She was the richest in her family after her grandfather... Can you beat that!! She made sure all her siblings went to school, and if anyone of them didn't have a thing for education, she'd see to it that that person has a business of his/her choice going on. She'd fund everything. She owned a motherless baby's home, where she'd keep kids thatare abandoned in her clinic. She'd buy things in bulk and give out to all of her relatives and any neighbor who comes crying. So abundant was the flow,so numerous were the goodies.

Things skyrocketed when Mother's boss died and she was to start heading the affairs of the hospital. The man's family didn't raise an eyebrow,they were comfortable with mother taking charge. But the other workers, they were far from pleased. They nursed grudges and made plans and it w as through them that I had a view of the other side of life. The other side of the wealth and riches that I was born into. Sandra patiently gave her listening hears as she encouraged her to co ntinue.

One fateful and life changing day, mother sent her driver to go get her lunch. She left home hurriedly that day, so she didn't make plans for lunch.The driver got the food back in no time and mother ate. In a couple ofminutes, things changed. She started feeling funny. She got dizzy and it was as if she swallowed a very tiny devil that was playing dangerously with her inside. She felt her lungs and intestine tear apart. She fell down. Darknesswas closing in on her already. She has been poisoned.

The people around tried to keep her stable, they didn't succeed. She was battling to stay alive. She was losing it really fast. News of th is calamity reached us at home and we were troubled. The next couple of days were trouble-filled. Mother was being taken from one hospital to another. None could fix her. They tried churches, mosques and traditional houses. No onecared that it is against our religious belief to take her to some places, but wejust needed her back. Anyhow! She didn't recover but I guess all the things they did to her everywhere they took her to, were the things that kept heaven's door locked for a while, she couldn't ente r. She wasn't a part of thisworld either. She was hanging in between both worlds. Someone soon suggested that they take her to villages nearby, there could be help waiting outside the border of our city. And away she

went.

.. And so, did goodfortune.

Life without mother started. Days turned to weeks. Weeks got pregnant and conceived months. Months grew and became years. Mother has been away for more than a year now and nothing has been heard of her. My sis and I were ignorant of what things were like w ith her. Like hung ry children, sadness came into our home with a truckload of minions and they fed on our once-booming barn of supposedly inexhaustible happiness, they went rogue on it and we were out of joy in no time. We soon exhausted all the goodies mother left behind and lack crept in. My funny wish to get sent out of school came true. countlessly. The fee became unaffordable. The teachers in school couldn't understand this terrible change in fortune. My English teacher called me one day to ask what w as happening in my family. Icouldn't say much. She hugged me really close and cried. There was no driver to take me to school anymore, so I started going with the school bus.

The school driver never asked for a dime until later. I eventually dropped out of school. Gosh, things were hard!

Until then, I didn't realize that Dayo, my supposed cousin is not actually my cousin, he is my blood brother. I couldn't accept that fact. I mean, how can my brother be thirteen long years older than I am? I later realized that after my parents birthed him, mother had issues conceiving another child. She was trying to make father's numerous penetrative efforts worth it, but it was like father's fluids were leaking out of her as soon as he poured in her but how? Father didn't hav e no chill, he went scouting for some lady outside, and got her pregnant. Guess what? That lady is mother's friend. Six months after he pumped his new mistress to some stomach swelling degree, mommahad me in her stomach as well. Remember I said father is jobless? Right! He was taking care of the woman with mother's money and when this predicament started, he built a house for himself and his mistress, on one of mother's lands and he didn't give a damn about us.

Dayo was trying to make ends meet somewhere outside ourcommunity, even before mother became a case, so he was rarely around– that's one of the reasons that made me give him the tag cousin without stress. Months after I clocked 9, mother's absence from home became 2years.My sister, Anu and I were instructed to stuff our boxes with all of ourbeautiful clothes, we had to go stay with my aunt and her family. She is one of mother's closest siblings. When life was still good, she used to comearound and she'd return with her bags filled to the very brim . She'd alwaysadmire my relationship with mother. Whenever mother is off duty at work and she's home, I'd always lean on her. I'd hold her and follow her all over the house. I was glued to her. And my aunt used to find that really amusing.

I wasn't expecting life to be anything but interesting in my aunt's place. Anu and I were treated well in our new house, of cos... aunt has no choice. But the special treatment didn't last for so long, soon she changed and I began todoubt if this was the same aunt that I knew.

Her first complaint was that I used to lean on her the way I used to do with mother. Why should that even be a problem? She said it's bad habit. And that it must stop. She'd insert that warning into my skull with a scream.

" Don't hold me. It's bad habit. And I won't accept that here!!!!!".

When we came in newly, we could eat what we wanted, even if aunt and her children ate something else. That stopped too. She said never again will she make two different meals in just one house. The logic behind that, I couldn't fathom. Anu started falling ill. Aunt would take her to one woman'splace next door for treatment. Not for once did she take her to a hospital. Grandma soon heard of the illness and she took Anu with her. And that's how I was alone with aunt and her family. She was a teacher in a public school near where she stays. I was bound for primary five before I dropped out earlier, my aunt knew this. She got me enrolled in her school and her class, primary four.

She got me a seat behind the class and mostly when she's teaching, she'd give me melon to pick so that we'd have it to eat when we return home.

When we return home, I'd go to her husband's farm to work. I wasn't used to this kind of life but I learned fast. She'd give her children my best clothes to wear. One of mother's friend that stays near my aunt's house noticed the unfair treatment and challenged her one day, she reminded my aunt of how things were like when mother was still good, and told her to treat me theway mother used to treat her, and stop treating me like a slave. Aunt toldher to mind her business and leave her house. She refused and was still talking when my aunt went inside, returned with a bucket of water and she emptied it on her. Oh mine, I felt bad for her. She use d to visit occasionallybefore this particular day, but she learnt her lesson. She never came back. Things got worse after her visit. During holidays, I'd hawk Kunu all over the street while her children would roam about the house, playfully. When other relatives visit, I'd go meet them when aunt is not watching and I'd ask for money. I'd make them promise not to tell aunt about it, but they didn't understand why. I used to get enough money this way so whenever aunt sends me hawking, I'd give the Kunu to be ggars, there used to be a lot of them, and I'd return home and give aunt the money I got from relatives. She'd think I sold out. They all stopped visiting later and I had to really sell. I'd often wash her clothes, her children's and her husband's. There w as a dayI complained. She slapped me so hard, so much that the world around meturned upside down. I bent my head to adjust to the new reversed shape ofthe world and in no time, it switched back to normal but it left me with a splitting headache and blood made its way into my eyes. That cleared outlater though. She'd always ask me if she 'sent my mother work'.

'Tell me, am I the one that poisoned your mother? She didn't teach you well,I'd help her!!'

Thoughts of mother would come into my bleeding heart. And I'd cry severally. I'd reminisce when I lay in bed. I concluded that mother died already but they didn't want me to know but I figured it out myself. I wantedto leave here but where to? Father alre ady sold most of mother's things. I heard he travelled to France and he now has more children with mother's friend that he married. He probably forgot that I'm existing. It's all good I understand so well. I'd sleep with tears in my eyes and wake up with w orries and aches.' Sandra's eyes were almost teary as she continued to listen to her heart touching story.

One bad day, I returned from the farm with aun t's husband. I was sotired. And dirty. Until now, I still had the privilege of bathing with warm water. I was brought up that way. But this day, aunt said I should go bathe with cold water. I used to think my skin would fall off if I ever try cold water.I tried explaining to aunt that there's no way I can do that. She screamed at me and said she'd make sure I do not sleep until I wash up with cold water.

I was too tired to stay on my feet. I removed my dirty cloth, sat on oneof the chairs in the sitting room and.... slept off in no time. I remember having a bad dream in which a masquerade was chasing me with a long whip.I slipped and the masquerade came really close, took u p the whip and slash!I felt the pain so much. Again, he raised the whip and slash! I wanted toscream but I couldn't then I tried to wake up. You know what I woke up to? aunt's beating. She's been beating me the whole time I was having a nicetime with the masquerade in my dream. Hers were the whipping I was feeling, not the Masquerade's . I ran for cover, she followed me and beat me even more. My offence? I slept off without bathing with cold water. I noticedthat the main door wasn't closed. With some sup er speed, I reached for it, drew it and ran out. Everywhere was so dark. She came ou tside and ordered me inside. I refused. She then told me she'd count 1 to 5 after which, if I'm not in, I'd never be.

'By the time I count 1 to 5 and you are not inside th is house, you'd never come inside again!!!! Come here and take your beating already' .

You know how a strong headed sinner would stay glued to his seat during an altar call, yeah right! I didn't flinch. But before she counted 5, I realized that she wasn't bluffing and that I won't go inside that house anymore if I miss out on this salvation call of hers. Gradually, I advanced towards her just as she said:

And she bolted her door. That sealed my fate. The night was so cold and scary. It was obviously close to midnight. I waited for a while then I started pleading. It was futile. Her husband didn't say a word either. I then decided to go to mother's friend that stays down the street. The one that got baptized the day she came to tell my aunt to be nicer to me .

I knocked on her door, she opened and after narrating my ordeal to her, with tears in her eyes, she told me there's nothing she can do because she's scared my aunt would come barking when she realizes that she took me in for the night, she said she swore to never be involved with her again in her life after the event that came up the other day. She told me to return to my aunt's place and that she'd let me in later. 'She can't be so heartless to leave you out in this dark and cold night'.

But she was wrong. I went to my aunt's house, knocked severally but got no response. Naked except for the pant I had on, I curled up in a corner and was staring blankly. The noisy clock in my aunt's parlor started chiming and it rang twelve times. It's 12 o'clock and I'm out here in the dark.

A thought came to my mind, and I embraced it. I decided to walk toone of my uncle's place. He stays quite far from here but I decided to payhim an ungodly hour visit. I got used to the road since I started my hawking business, but I avoid plying this particular route because it leads back homeand I'd hate to be mocked by the children that knew when life was good forme, so I don't go this way ever. But tonight, I did. Without shoe or cloth, I embarked on this journey. Mad people hovered across the street.

Homelesspeople strayed in corners. Gamblers were still up. Dipsomaniacs with heavystench of alcohol were finding their home. This night is mine, so, so mine.

I got to my uncle's three storey building, he has two wives. Each owns a floor but he stays in the topmost one. I went straight to his and landed blows that startled him up in seconds. He asked who was knocking at such odd hour. I mentioned my name. What he said next made me smile. Immediately I mentioned my name, he said 'God forbid. It can't be you'.

'Open your door and you'd find out if it's me or not'.

He was silent for a while. Then, his door creaked quietly. I felt his eyeson me. He locked the door again and went back in. He said:

'Esther, it's, you. And you are n ot wearing anything. This is strange. I won'tlet you in until I'm sure you are not a ghost'.

'I'd be if you don't open soon. Your sister sent me out. I just want tosee my mother. Tonight, you'd take me to her. If she's dead, I want to see her grave. Everything must end.... to-to-to-ni-ght'. Tears choked me really hardbefore that last word could leave my mouth.

My uncle opened his door and I narrated all that has been happening.He never visited me in my Aunt's place since the day he drove my sister and I there. The few other relatives who used to come around stopped, I was simply abandoned. When I was done talking, he left to get his wives. Thetime was 1:30AM now. His wall clock told me so.

He returned with his wives and they brought food. I ate till I couldn't anymore. I was digging into the food recklessly. Believe me, by the time I was done eating, they were all in tears. The way I ate, told th em what life hasbeen for me since mother left 4 years ago. I noticed he was getting dressed. He told his wives to go do the same. He came towards me and said we'd go to my aunt's place right now and pack all my things. I'd return with him though. I was glad. I asked him where mother's grave was. His answer stunned me wildly.

'Your mother is not dead.'

I couldn't believe what he just said. He then explained to me how mother has been away in a neighboring city, where she eventually got fixed. But she's been recuperating ever since and she's been told to not return herefor now. And that since father already sold all we had, there's actually nothing to return to. But she'd be good enough and everything will be fine.If this news came before the meal, I'd be too filled and I'd not have tasted anything. Not even water. He said Anu has been with grandma and that we'dgo see mother when she's a lot better. With my uncle – the bearer of the bestnews I've heard in years, and his two wives, we rode in my Uncl e's car and went to my aunt's house.

The night was still so dark when we got there. My uncle jumped out ofhis car and almost tore down my aunt's door with knocks.

'Open this door this very moment. Open it!!!!'.

My aunt knew his voice, so she was sure I wasn't the one. She opened up after a while and...... As expected, a war erupted. She blamed my uncle for neglecting me ever since, my uncle came up with his perfect defense-he's been busy taking care of my mother and seeing to other things. He said not once did my aunt ask him about mother's situation , instead she's been treating me like a child she picked up from the r oadside. Authoritatively, he instructed her to go pack my things for I'd be leaving her house this moment.She didn't say any other word. She went in and returned with like four rags wrapped in a smelly black nylon. My uncle opened his mouth. 'I personally drove the girl and her Sister here when we decided that they should start staying with you. Her own clothes filled up three big boxes. What hap penedto everything? Answer me!!'. 'That's all she has left now.' she replied coldly.

My uncle picked up the nylon bag and with so much effort, hurled it ather face and he stormed out. His two wives and I followed.

My uncle took me in and life changed. Again. It was similar to whatthings were like before mother left. My sister came in two days after Iarrived my uncle's place. When she saw me, she jumped at me and I almostfell. We were locked in a very tight embrace. We were crying on each other'sshoulders. We were that way for minutes. No on e separated us, no one couldtry. For the first time in years, I felt at ease and totally at peace.

My Sister returned to grandma's place but she visits regularly. Like two months after I arrived uncle's place, he returned one day and told mesomething that made me scream loudly. His wives came out, they heard mynoise and they were very scared. uncle just told me we'd be visiting mothertomorrow. The only way to express my joy was the way I just did. My uncle explained to his wives the reason why I coughe d out that noise. They smiledthereafter. Anu came that evening, uncle brought her, she'd be coming withus tomorrow. We couldn't sleep. Tell me,

How could we?

Mother was different now. She was so lean and w hen I saw her, I must confess, I was so scared, I almost ran out of that room. Dayo was in the roomas well. Anu didn't feel what I was feeling. She ran blindly to mother and hugged her. Everyone was looking at me. I couldn't move my legs. I was too scared. I made a conscious effort to unglue my l egs one after the other. It worked. I moved towards my mother and she had he r arms open. From that distance, I could see that lonely tear that made way for others in her eyes. I increased my pace and I was in her arms; the best place to ever be in the world. Anu joined in the embrace, after hesitating for a while, Dayo joined us. And together, we were letting out several pitches and tones of tears.

We had to leave her - trust me, it took all the pleas in the world to do so.

They said we'd return next week. Finally. Here would be home till way later when she'd be good enough to make a triumphant return back to where home used to be. We moved in with mother later.

Things were far from what they used to be lik e but we were happy.

Mother could work now. She got a job in a small clinic in this town. Withlittle support from my uncle and Dayo's contributions, we were living good.We returned back to our initial home. The only property father didn't sell. But it's been abandoned for so long. We cleaned up and gave it a look similar to what it used to have. The hospital where mother was wo rkingbefore, she was poisoned already folded up. While we were away, the driver confessed to the crime of poisoning mother. He m entioned some othernames as well. Whatever they did to them all, we don't know. I was expecting to hear father's name pop up, but it didn't. I keep wondering whyhe acted that way. Dayo told me something that I'd never forget. He said,father never paid any of our fees. He never acted like a father. But forimpregnating mother, he owes him a bottle of coke - that and nothing else. I don't owe him a thing, that bottle of coke he'd get from

Dayo should be enough for his callous self. I told mother I'd never forgive her sister, and Iswear, I'd never!

CHAPTER NINE

THE CHOICE OF LOVE

Segun's story is one that would touch the heart of any human being. His father died just when he got Celebrated his thirteenth years birthday. His father was a successful farmer, he had a large plantation and was able to provide for his family adequately. The family wa s a happy one, Segun had two other siblings who were younger than himself.

Few months before his father's death, there was a misunderstanding between his father's extended family, his grandfather had three wives. Segun's father was the first child of his mother, the second wife of Segun's grandfather. The family would often clash on land related issues after the death of his grandfather, and they would soon go diabolical about it. It was during another conflict like this that his father fell ill. A lot of money was spent on his sickness, but the doctors would not just figure out what the problem is, His father eventually died in the process, introducin g them to a new phase of life.

Segun would easy fall into the class of children whom the cliché 'born with a silver spoon' would describe. 5ft 9inches tall, fair-skinned, black hair, dimpled-face and very intelligent. Everything seems to go well with him until the calamity hit his family- a blow expertly aimed at them by fate itself.Now in year two, he left cl ass one day and was returning home when his mother called him; she was in tears, the last time he heard her cry like this was during his father's burial, she's been really strong since then.

It took her minutes to finally put herself together and tell hi m what prompted the urgent call. She informed him that Sade, his younger Sister was brought home dead, she was reportedly returning home from school when she mysteriously fell down and dropped dead .

Segun was devastated. This was like a nightmare to him. Life became tough as his mother could not go to her husband's farm anymore out of fear that charms might have been placed on the farms by her husband 's relative, life became so though for the family. Segun's younger brother, Kola, was attending one of the prestigious and highly rated high-school until evil start to reign in the family, he then had to withdraw to a school with less charges just so there'd be enough fund to take care of Segun till he graduates, get a lucrative job and restore wealth to the fa mily, funny how we as humans make plans without having a clue whatsoever what awaits us.

Segun was doing well in school and despite the financial crises in his family, his schooling didn't stop, he just wasn't as comfortable as he used to be but he could still afford the annual rent he pays for his apartment off - campus. Due to Segun's experience, his relationship suffered.

He had always preferred to be quiet and not relate with anyone. The only friend he has was his roommate, Bode who was studying Mechatronics engineering. This also made him not to even consider any romantic relationship with any girl as he really doesn't care about anyone at the moment but for the survival of his mother and the only sibling left.

His mother would tease him every time he was home telling him of how much she desires a daughter-in-law, he'd just smile and walk away. His best friend, Bode was his exact opposite, one hell of a Casanova, that dude! People would often wonder how they get along, but it was no big deal since Bode would not bring in girls when Segun is around, moreover, Segun spends most of his days in the library.

Bode would always keep his business with women away from Segun'sface and this was why they rarely had issues. He'd always tell Segun to prepare for that lady that'd smear him all over with feelings; the latter wouldpull out of any talk like that quickly, the lady came around eventually. With just two months away from his second year, second semester exams, his firstencounter with Sandra.

Sandra was touched after hearing Segun story, deep within her heart, shewants to be there for him.

CHAPTER TEN

THE DEVIL HAS FALLEN

Adex had become a different person entirely, he now spends most time alone away from the other members of the wolf fraternity, Sandra's words never stopped ringing in his hears. He was alone under a tree with a book in his hand, yes, a book titled *how to win friends and influence people* by Dale Canagie. He now reads about relationships and friendship he really wan ted to be a different person, he wanted to stop being Adex the Wolf Lord, in fact, he had been missing the fraternity meetings to the dismay of the whole cult group, who still wait patiently for the devil's return, the fearful Adex.

As he was reading and meditating under the tree, Collins came to himout of nowhere with a dagger in his hand. Adex for the first time trembl ed, the whole world knew Collins as Collins, a gentleman with a lovablepersonality but to the people of the dark worlds, he is 'C -Death', the mostpotent agent of destruction of the blades. Adex had neglected his usualrituals and metaphysical empowerment. Collins had met him in the wr ongtime. 'Cee, to what do I owe this visit?' Collins laughed hysterically. 'Ade', he called his name emphatically, 'the number one gladiator of the Wolves, theone who strikes fear into even the kings of the Jungle, it's a pity how you have become so weak. Well, you made a mistake the moment you decided tosnatch the woman I love away from me and the penalty f or your deed is

death.' He aimed the dagger at him, strikes him with it and Adex fell to the ground. Collins feeling victorious left the scene. 'now, Sandra would be mine' he said to himself.

CHAPTER ELEVEN

C-DEATH: REVELATION

Collins lost both his poor parents to strange illnesses before he was 15years old, for a child that young, surviving alone wasn't easy one bit, but he did it. He was four when his father died so he didn't miss him much, bu t itwas right in his arms that his mother drew in her last breath, he buried herhimself after saying a quick prayer over her body. His father's house at Cuernavaca Mexico City, was where he was before Nigeria came callingseveral years after his parent's painful exit from this world. He'd go intotown, get some shady deals done and pile up quid till he had enough moneyto cater for himself and school since he knew none of his relatives.

After school he decided to base in the city of Ibadan. Surviving here wasn't easy for him bu t he was managing till he was good enough to own an apartment at Main street Town . He'd go deep into the neighborhood, put his ears to the ground for anyone seeking justice on some persons who need to be treated right after carrying out an action that ju st don't seem right.

All he needs is the victim's picture, address and essentially- money. With the right information, he could go into the Aso rock and return with the President right inside his pocket.

The demise of his parents had exposed him to the other side of the lawway so early in his life; killing, beating, robbing, burgling is all he could do for the right pay and information. Though he was able to conceal his real identity from many while he was in school . The early taste of adulthood

which nature shoved his way made him part ways wit h his conscience. He has ears everywhere who ring him up if anyone needs to be taken care of, the proper way. His high level of intelligence and animal brutality made hima fan of any weapon but a gun, he hates the word 'trigger'. He owns a closet in his one room apartment at Main Street Town, the closet is a collection ofvarious shapes, sizes and lengths of knife- his favorite weapon, and a big bottle of concentrated acid which he uses occasionally. He handles a knife way better than Leonardo Da Vinci handled the brush while painting thepopular Monalisa. He smokes like a chimney, there's always a stick of cigarette in-between his fingers, he stopped laughing, never.

Since Sandra, he never cared about any lady anymore. He met Cindy astripper, during one of his night out at a club in the island. He'd lost interestin women, but the night Cindy came up to him to ask if he needs a lady to help him scratch his back, he decided he could use an encounter with her. He's not been sexually active in a while, he has never had a steady girlfriendand this night, it dawned on him that he could use a rel ease. Every moveCindy made in luring him, only succeeded in ripping his zippers apart as hisrod pushed aggressively at it. Cindy had a well carved out body, all bodycontours and shape was expertly lined out and she got to Collins withoutstress that night. He flanked down a cab which rode them to his apartment. Dragging Cindy along noisily, he raced up the stairs. The doorman jolted back to life for he was gradually dozin g off until Collins came rushing in, helooked at his watch and the time was exactly 11:55pm, he had five moreminutes before he retreats to bed.

Collins kicked open his door and went for a quick shower while Cindyundressed. He returned to the room with the towel on his waist all he had on. The sight of Cindy on his bed gave him a feeling of violent sexual longing, she put her finger in her mouth and rubbed it with spit and said

'You ain't shy boy, are you? Come on already. I don't have all night and I st illhave plans to make a couple of dough b efore the day gets darker'.

'You'd be screaming soon I promise, I'm so not going easy on you'. 'Let's seewhat you have bloke'.

He unwrapped the towel and his already hard rod came into full view, Cindy drew in a breath and whispered 'Now that's some meat you have'. She spread her legs thereafter, inviting him in fully. They rolled each other up into a big ball of passion and the movement his waist made was pretty fast enough to outrun a flash of lightning. Cindy couldn't help but scream despite her age long experience of sleeping with several men.

Collins was rough and she loved it, for he drove

her wild. He climaxed and rolled away from her as he made effort to catch his breath. Cindy decided to slash her price just so she'd stay the night 'Fifteen box boy and I'dbe yours all night, that's way less than I'd make if I leave'.

'You pretty, you ain't got gold around it, I'm spitting ten, if you desire a box more, use the door'. 'Easy, you do it good no doubt and that's why I'm goingstay. Ten it is then'.

They spent the entire night in each other's arms after some more rounds. By the time morning came, there was an insane chemistry between them. He brought her coffee and that got to her, no one's treated her tha t way in a while. They had a quick chat, got horny again, kissed, penetration occurred, they had a shower together and they had a deal to meet at the club later at night. He had to go check if a job was available, the last he had was last week and it was smooth as usual but he needs one again for he's fast running low on cash. He paid Cindy and together they bounced out of his apartment. Just before they parted ways, his phone rang. One of his ears in town has sure got a job, they don't summon unless duty c alls. He grinned happily as he clicked the green button .

He hung up and his face was littered with nervous blushes. '...and boy, why get so ripe?' Cindy questioned. 'Last I checked, I don't answer to no one. See ya later'.

CHAPTER TWELVE

NEMESIS

He replied and flanked down a cab. 'How fast can you get to Williams Street from here?'. He asked the old driver. '20 minutes son' 'Make it 10 minutes, I'd double your pay'. The driver looked at the rear mirror a nd displayed his brown dentition in a fake sm ile. 'Why not!, Shall we?'. 'Set sail and fly oldie, the day's getting short'.

The driver gave the engine life and flew away. Collins thought about the call he got. He's been waiting for a deal this big since fo rever, this might just be it. Ears on the street said a rich dude's ready to vomit five hundred thousand naira for an elimination. He ain't toying with this, not today not ever. Traffic was good and he was in Williams Street in 10 minutes as promised. He paid the man, alighted and he was off to meet his caller. The terms of the job was clear-perfect and fast, Tomorrow latest. He doesn't do deals this fast but for this amount, he'd do anything.

An aggrieved rich client Johnson, needs someone eliminated due to anissue which came up as a result of a girl he lost. The victim's name's Ben, Collin's to take out the girlfriend Janet as well. Jane was Johnson's girlfriend until she took his money and packed in with Ben, Jason won't let them go away with this. Collins was thinking of how to go about the mission, he gulped a cup of scotch and lit a cigarette. He heard his vibrant mind whisperto him that he just might need Cindy for this. She'd take care of Jane while he fixes Ben. He doesn't know her yet, he can't trust her b ut he's willing to

risk it. He'd meet her tonight and talk to her. In two days', time, he'd be smiling to the bank if all goes well. He left Williams Street and he hurried up

back to home.

Johnson demanded that both Ben and Jane be killed, that wasn't odd just that he demanded a very smooth job and he needed it done within a very short time frame. Collins had been smoking since he got back, the ash tray beside him was a mess already. He poured himself scotch and felt it walk lazily down his chest.

His phone rang, he picked up and his knuckle turned white when he heard what he was told on the phone. It was Johnson who called him, he justmade the deal almost so impossible but he promised to double the pay if all goes well. He told Collins that Ben and Jane would be going on a date at Royal Class dish at Mayor Street tomorrow and he needs him to strike them there; murder on a date.

The time was 5:30 pm, when he left his room after he took a shower. He has plans for tomorrow night already and also a rol e for Cindy in the set-up. He rushed down to Strip club hoping to see Cindy around, he wasn'tdisappointed, she was in the lounge. She smiled wryly when she saw him buthe didn't smile back and this froze out the smile on her face. He grabbed herhands and said.

'It appears I have a job which c an put a thousand dollars on your t abletomorrow. That's about the total amount you make in 6 months. 'Now don'tmake me wet pretty boy, that's a lot for an underpaid stripper like me, I could leave here and seek l ife elsewhere with that amount'.

'See you spending the money you haven't ev en been paid yet. Save your boring plans for yourself. No work's easy for such an amount.' 'I'm down for whatever pretty boy'. 'We'd find out soon enough. How about we go to my place and I fill you in properly?'. 'No charges tonight, bang away'.

They got to his apartment and the first thing she did was peel off everypiece of cloth on her, she was stark naked. She moved away from the bed and got herself a cigarette from the pack on the table, she poured herself a scotch after dropping two ice cubes in a tumbler. Collins could only stare as she hopped around the room boasting of her naked beauty. His face was expressionless and cold, way colder than an iceberg. Pinky sat opposite hi m but he ignored the urge to pounce on her immediately. There's business to worry about and he's disciplined enough to not mix it with pleasure. She'd take out Jane, while he'd handle Ben. She asked what the total earning was but he didn't say. She figu red out in her head, that a job from which sh e'd earn so much would earn Cindy even more. She could use all the amount she can get from this deal. He didn't notice the look of greed which she hid behind her bitchy smile.

They spent the entire night discussing how to get things done tomorrow night. When she heard that they'd go on a date to the restaurant, the Royal Class dish. Her chest almost exploded with joy, she's been waiting for this all her life. That's one of the most expensive Inns around town, the serene environment around it was the height of its advantage over all others.They'd sit close to Ben and Jane at the date. She'd mess with her heels, tilt the table and send all that is on it on their body and suggest that Jane follows her into the toilet to clean-up, she'd take her out with a sil ent shot inthere. He on the other hand would take Ben into the male toilet as well and get his job done. That sounded so easy to him but he was ready for surprises that might arise. Cindy said she owns a pistol, she'd use that, he'd get his knife and tie up his side of the deal. Her contributions and composure stunned him, he was getting attracted to her gradually. They jumped into the bed at 1:35am. She sat on him, led his hand to her breast, he didn't cup it, he didn't move, he only stared. 'Not tonight girl'. He said and lifted her naked body off himself. Pinky was hurt, no man has turned down her sexual advances but Collins just did. In the darkness of the room, she smiled wickedly and decided to make her plans too, she's got a surprise for him, she could use the entire night ruminating. Collins shifted to the edge of his bed and stared at the ceiling with a fixed gaze, his whole life could change after this deal. He wondered if he could trust Cindy, he'd pay her well and that should rid her of greed, he forgot that anyone who attempts to satisfy a woman's greed for money is just as hopeless as he who is trying to fill a basket up with water.

Morning rolled in very fast, he could barely sleep. The bag under her eyes told him that she was up for a while as well. He had to go to the Inn where all would go down later tonight to get familiar with things, she'd go with him. Jason would be waiting at the end of Elizabeth Street to hand him hispay after the job. He'd Park beside the traffic light opposite Pony stores.He'd get him a car for the job, which he's due to return after the date. He lefthome with Cindy and off to Elizabeth Street. He sighted a suitable spot topark the car Johnson would give him for the job later, now he'd go in andcheck for another exit asides the main one just in case things roll out of control. He spotted one and he was so happy. Cindy would escape throughthe same exit as well and they'd meet in the car. All was set a nd the night drew nigh quickly.

They returned to his apartment and made final plans. Johnson called him tocome pick up the car and fed him half of his pay. With a little extra to get himself some wears for the night. He inquired about Collin's plans, Collinsonly told him that the only thing he should worry about is to be where he should to hand him his full pay later. Johnson was impressed, Collins stankof confidence and that's admirable. He left Johnson and went to a store to get a well sown suit and something for the girl too. He returned home with apocket full of notes and a bag stuffed with wears. Cindy wasn't in when hegot back and the time now was 5:25pm, he needs her to go over her lines all over again. She told him she'd go get he r pistol but shouldn't be away forlong. He was getting uneasy, a knock whic h definitely was Cindy's calmedhim down. He gave her the stuffs he got her, she was so excited and kissed him gently, he didn't respond. From the two hundred thousand Jason gavehim, he gave her a hundred thousand. He'd give her one fifty when theyreturn at night.

Her face lit up with euphoria as she rubbed her face with thedough, she imagined what it'd be like to own the entire pay to herself. They'd leave home in an hour and thirty minutes time. They rehearsed allthe plans again, it was perfect. He went into his closet and picked up arather short knife with a wooden handle and curved blade, sheathed it and he placed it inside his suit. Cindy was about pouring herself a drink when heturned, he barked at her to stop for he needs her to be so active and n otunder any influen ce whatsoever. Cindy smiled and let go of the bottle andthe cup which was half-full, she ripped off her cloth and went in to theshower room. Collins downed the glass and lit a cigarette. He'd get a showersoon too and they'd leave at exactly 8 o'clock. He was nervous and he didn'tunderstand why. For the first time since his mother died, he said a prayer, a very short one.

He parked his car somewhere outside the Key West Harbor Inn , he looked at Pinky who was gorgeously dressed in a blue short gown and pearl accessories. He said to her 'You look so good, you know... Huh?'. 'Even the devil knows that, let's roll pretty boy'.

She was charming and he felt the violent urge to have a qu ickie in the car before they leave, she saw desire in hi s eyes and she winked 'Not now pretty boy, so not now'.

Collins alighted and went to open her door. She stepped out like a real lady, clutching tightly to her bag inside which was her gun. The security at the Inn, opened the door with a bow and the restau rant was in view. Ben andJane were in already and the table next to them was occupied, this annoyed Collins. They had to settle for a table w hich was like three away from their victims. From here, he could see all that was happening with Ben and Jane.He ordered fried rice, Cindy ordered the same. They'd get things done in like10minutes time. He could see sweat gathering on Pinky's forehead, he eyedher furiously and she wiped it out, trying so hard to relax. He touched hissuit to feel the knife, he felt good after that. There's no leaving here without knocking those two out. He looked at Jane and Ben again, they were smilingthat very moment, he's only seen their pictures and, in his imaginations,, hehas painted them dead severally, soon they'd be out f or real. He couldn't eat,Cindy was done, he whispered quietly, 'Three more minutes'. 'Roger thatpretty boy, I'm all set '.

The hands of the clock ran down the face of the clock l ike a fat woman would sprint down a terrace; slowly and annoyingly. Collins had his eyes on his watch, drama time is now- 9:30pm. Without saying a word, Cindy stood

up and walked towards Ben and Jane's table, Collins
watched nervously, ready to spring up to play his own
role. Now at close range, Cindy put her full weight on
her heels and it broke perfectly. She struggled to gain
balance and turned the table over in the process.
Carter and Jane were s tunned and so furious

'Hell no, if you can't handle heels go barefooted!
What nonsense!'. Jane saidas she stood up and sent
her palm on an errand to Cindy's face. The slap was
loud and it hurt Cindy who had her hands in the air
ready to land Jane a veryhot slap in retaliation. That'd
jeopardize the mission but right now, slappingJane
was the only thing on Cindy's mind, she was so
hurt. Collins who wasclose-by caught her hand
midair and that saved the day. The restaurant was in
disarray, everyone turned t o their direction. Collins
apologized and said

'She's with me and it's clearly an accident, I'm so sorry
about this.Let's handle this calmly.'

Ben was a mess but not as big a mess as Jane. He was calm now and heplacated Jane who wouldn't stop fuming.

'It's all alright gentle man'. Turning to Pinky he added   'and I'm sorry aboutthe slap, I'm sure it was impulsive'.

Calm by now as well and so glad Collins stopped her from slapping Jane,

Cindy smiled and offered to go clean Jane up in the toilet.
Jane

saidarrogantly

'You have a lot of cleaning-up to do just so you know'.

'I won't complain' Cindy retorted.

'Hope you do not mind if I offer to tidy you up too sir'.

Collins said.'I'm fine, don't bother'. He said.

A look of shock appeared on Collin's face, this dude just can't say no mehn.

'I insist sir, help my conscience. I'd feel so bad if you don't let me do this'. Ofcourse, he'd feel bad, so bad. Carter smiled and said 'You are such a good man, alright let's do this'. 'Exactly!' Collins screamed. happily.

Jane and Cindy stared at the two men. Just then, on e of the waiters came around and said he'd handle the cleaning -up thingy, the hotel has made provision for incidents like this but it was Carter who spoke thi s time.

'Just fix the mess on the floor, we'd take care of ourselves'.Cindy wasabout exploding with fear, she was that scared of the waiter's offer. They left the restaurant and headed for the toilet. A panel divided the female andmale compartment, as the ladies went into theirs, Collins said to Cindy,

'Make it snappy'. There was a message in it for her which neither Carter norJane understood. 'I sure will'. She rep lied.

Cindy and Jane got into the toilet but there was someone else there, a blonde was re-applying her makeup. 'Shit!!' she said aloud. Jane looked at her and asked surprisingly 'What's the problem?'. 'It's nothing'. She said and hid the scary blushes that was invading her face. Just then the blonde packedher bag and went out, Cindy turned the lock as she did. Jane was suddenly alert, 'What are you doing'.

The vicious look on Cindy's face made her shake. Cindy reached for her gun in the bag and in a millisecond, she perforated Jane's chest. The shottore her heart apart and she fell dow n with a thud that alerted Collins in theother room. She went near her body and stamped her ribcage real hard 'That's for the slap bitch'. She said and spat on her.

Collins was lucky with Ben, they had the toilet alone. He was waiting to hear Cindy leave the lady's toilet before he tampered with Ben. Cindy's shot was silent but Jane's thud wasn't. Collins and Ben looked at the direction of the sound, Ben was distracted for a while, and like a serpent, Collins crawled in behind him, brought out his knife, held Ben from behind and with a sharp reflex, he pierced his heart with a stab, removed th e knife and dug it in again, Ben drew in fast breath as he felt his last pain. Collins dropped him on the ground

'Nice perf, I should say'. He said to Ben's dead body as he wiped out the blood stain on the knife using Ben's shirt, then he sheathed it and returned it to his pocket. He left the toilet about the same time

Cindy turned the lock on her way out of t he lady's. She already pulled out her surviving heel so she'd walk freely. Collins turned the lock as well just sono one would see the body easily. Before anyone would break

down the door,they'd be so far gone. In quick strides ,
they hurried to the exit door behind the building.
There was no security there as expected. It was not
until they got inside the car that they spoke. Collins
spoke first 'Went well?' 'So, well'. 'Let's go meet that
bloke for the remaining pay'. 'I hope he'd be there'. 'He
sure will'.

Jason's car was parked right where it should be. Collins
went to meet him, he's been eager. He tapped the
screen twice, Jason pushed a butt on and the window
went down 'Done'.

'Here'. he said and gave Collins the balance.'You'd get
the car in the morning , Safe'.

He went back into the car, smiled at Cindy and he drove home, they didn't say a word to each other.

The night was cold and the cloud stared intently at all with its bulgy eyes which is the moonlight.

Collins walked in with Cindy, he pinned her ag ainst the wall and ate deep into her mouth, he was kissing her with so much energy and he pressed his genitals against hers. She was frigid and so he retreated. He reached for two glasses, he filled both up and said teasingly,

'What were you saying about getting drunk earlier?'.

He dropped the bag containing the money on the table. He made to remove his suit and there was Cindy with a gun to his head. He smiled and hid his shock.

'Are you for real?' 'I'm not sharing this money with your ass'. She saidgreedily.

'You don't want to do this'. 'Of course, I want to, now shove the bag overhere'.

Collins was thinking fast but he couldn't think s traight.

'Don't try to be smart pretty boy, I swear I 'm going to blow you apart'. Hesaw this coming but he was unprepared, he could see that she was going to pull that trigger. Now he'd die with a bullet in his chest, of all things to kill him- a gun is just forbidden. He made to reach for his knife but Cindy wasfast, she squeezed the trigger and the bullet hit him hard but the shot only nicked his heart, if not, he'd have died on the spot but he was still breathing and he saw Cindy reach for the bag. With all t he energy he could muster, heput his hand inside his suit and brought out his knife.

Cindy had her face on the money and her back to Collins, so she didn'tsee him struggle to do one last thing. She zipped the bag and she attempted to carry it, then she felt something sink into the back of her neck, Collins finally threw the knife and it went in so deep just inches below her skull. The bag dropped first then her body followed.

Printed in Great Britain
by Amazon